A Tribute To My Father

Everything is Italian

By

Marco Perugini

TABLE OF CONTENTS

INTRODUCTION

Salvatore and Carmella

Sal, Carmella, Sal, Marco

This book is in memory of my father, Salvatore Perugini. He played such a major role as the patriarch of our family. Sal was born June 27, 1930, in Pontelondolfo, Benevento, Italy and came to the United States in 1954 at the age of 24 and became a U.S. citizen.

Sal had many endeavors as a Carbinieri on the Italian Riviera and trained and worked as a Chef in Switzerland before settling in Oakville, CT, where he lived with family and friends who had already made the journey west.

Sal first worked in a factory to generate some income and eventually started his own asphalt/paving and trucking company.

He then met my mother, Carmella Marie Perugini, an opera singer, who quickly became the love of his life. They married on March 9, 1957, purchased a home and had two sons:

Salvatore Jr. and myself/Marco.

Sal moved into the restaurant industry in 1965, and this would be his final and longest-lasting business, other than some real estate holdings. He and a partner opened the first A &W Root Beer Drive-In in CT.   It was a great success through the seventies.

April 7, 1983, Perugini's Italian Restaurant in Wolcott, CT was founded as owner and Chef, along with my mother, brother and myself. The restaurant was a staple in the town for 23 years.

My father was a world traveler. It was one of his many hobbies, so to speak. He was an incredible and avid hunter, earning him the nickname- 'The Rifleman.' He also loved to gamble, especially horseracing and was an avid card player; poker is at the top of his list. He also took countless trips to Las Vegas and Atlantic City.

He traveled back and forth to Pontelondolfo on a regular basis, spending time at our family's home there in the mountains of southern Italy. My Dad continued this until the age of 88.

As he got older, his garden became one of his biggest passions. His plants were incredible, and we'd laugh and say to him," Is this some kind of nuclear waste site?" They absolutely dwarfed the plants in my garden!

My Dad had his own way of doing and saying things that you just could not forget-he was truly one of a kind.

As I write this, he has been gone for a little over two years now. As a family, we are constantly quoting him. My kids are always texting things that Grandpa said, or he would do. He absolutely adored his grandchildren and considered my wife to be the daughter that he always wanted.

My two sons and my daughter looked up to him like he was the second coming of Jesus Christ [laugh], and it was amazing to watch! They never refused an ask from him, even if they were busy with school or life, and he never refused them anything. He was there for us, no matter what was needed.

While I had thought about writing a book about my family, Italian immigrants, my forte was the restaurant business and not writing. However, on a recent trip to visit my grandson in CT, I was quoting my Dad as usual, and my son-in-law suggested I write a book of Grandpa's hysterical quotes, the things he used to say and his way of reasoning and stories. Everything is Italian! He used to tell us when we were kids there were two kinds of people in this world…Italians and those who want to be Italians.

I hope you enjoy the compilation of micro-stories to follow.

THE TOE

I get a call one day from my Dad, [most days at this point, along with many visits at my door]. This was a call that went as follows:

'Marc, can you come over here please?' in his thick Italian accent.

[We lived only one house over on our street] 'I cut a piece of meat off my fucking toe.'

When I got there and walked in, he was sitting in his recliner; it looked like a crime scene [laugh]. There was

blood everywhere on the carpet, on the tile floor, on the chair, on him…

ME: 'Oh my God, Dad, what the hell happened!???'
DAD: 'I was trying to cut my Goddamn toenails, and I cut a piece of meat off, [laughs], Motherfucker!'

I quickly began patching up the injured toe. So now the problem is that he used to take blood thinners for Afib. The piece that was missing from the end of his toe was a complete nightmare to fix [laugh]. There was no sense in going to the ER, as there was nothing to stitch closed, and second, my Dad would never go in the first place, so I finally got the bleeding to stop after some time and bandaged up the toe.

The next problem was to keep him from walking on it for a while. He was constantly on the move, even in his late 80's. Within an hour or so, he was at my house, of course, not listening to anything I had said and within minutes, the

6

bleeding had started again, his sock was soaked with blood, and we had to start all over again!

I remember another foot incident where there was something wrong with one of his toes going under the other toe. My Dad, being the creative person that he was, decided to cut a hole in his shoe so the toe was able to have more room 'to breathe' [laugh]

DAD'S MEDICAL TERMINOLOGY & OTHER SAYINGS

We would laugh at my father's terminology for a lot of things, in a good way of course, as he had a way with his own pronunciation and making everything sound Italian, even though it was the furthest thing from Italian.

For instance, the common high fiber drink to help with constipation, **Metamucil**, became 'meta- muchillay.'

Antibiotics for infections were always called 'Antibiotic,'

And **Asprin,** for fever and pain, was **Asperine**

[which actually are the proper Italian spelling and pronunciations].

Ibuprofen, the common pain and fever reliever, was called,

'Ibu-profer-ine'.

CO Q10, a supplement for the heart, was just 'The Q10'.

Stool Softeners: If he decides to use them, 'I just take ah the 'soft stool.'

OTHER SAYINGS

My Dad had a few classic sayings that he often used, which always made us laugh at his delivery and the way he said things.

When he wanted to get rid of extra 'stuff' that was no longer useful, he would say, **'Throw these junks out,'** or if a house has too many decorative ornaments in their yard, **'Look at all the junks this guy has.'**

If my Dad could sense tension in the house when he would come over, he would put his hand on your shoulder and say, **'Don't fight. You kits [kids] got to love each other.'**

Our family always says *'I love you'* in our house, especially before we leave to go somewhere or to say goodnight. If my kids said, I love you, Grandpa or my wife told him she loves him as he is leaving to go home, his reply is always, **'Thank you.'**

When Dad didn't understand a piece of mail that he got or needed help with something, he would say, **'Give me a favor.'**

THE SUPER PERFECTA AT GREAT MOUNTAIN RACE TRACK

My father was an extremely smart man. He was an avid gambler, loved playing cards, and loved Casinos and rolling dice.

His favorite was horse racing.

Back in the fabulous 70s, he and his friends would go to Green Mountain horse track in Vermont at least a couple of nights a week. Yes, they made the two-or-so-hour drive to this not-so-great track [laugh].

If you don't know about betting wagers, there is the perfecta, the trifecta, win, place, show and more. There was a particular wager that they used to run at Green Mountain called the Super Perfecta. I honestly don't remember how this wager was different from the others, but as the story goes, it paid much more.

Somewhere along the line, my father, a very knowledgeable handicapper, developed a habit of not checking his tickets after placing one of his bets.

One particular evening, Sal hit the Super Perfecta, which paid $19,500.00. However, when he went to the window to collect his winnings, he had not checked his ticket when he originally placed the bet. The guy behind the window had given him the wrong numbers and, of course, had no idea the numbers were wrong.

My Dad went back to the same window, the same man, to collect his money. When the man looked at the ticket, he told my father it was *not* a winner. Needless to say, this ignited a volcanic eruption inside my father. He began arguing with the man, and when he told my father there was nothing he could do, he reached through the cage and proceeded to pull the man through it, intending to cause physical harm to him

[laugh].

Naturally, this caused quite a ruckus; security was called immediately, and my father and his henchmen were escorted out and off the grounds. To hear him tell this story over the years, always got big laughs.

THE BEAR

Sal was an incredible hunter, both big and small game. His intention was not just for the sport, but we were taught at a young age to respect nature and use the animal as a bounty for our dinner table.

Dad was an amazing marksman who never missed. His co-hunters gave him the name *'The Rifleman'*. [Upon his passing, I had it tattooed on my arm in his honor.]

As the years went on, the focus became a big game, as it did with my brother, my two sons and myself.

In 1967, on a hunting trip to Maine with his cousin Joe, they would later become local celebrities.

A few days into the trip, Joe bagged a 200-pound buck and my father a 420-pound black bear.

At that time, bear hunting was not yet a thing. This bear, along with his weight, stood over seven feet tall. They needed to find a few locals to help them get their large prey out of the woods. Needless to say, it took several hours and now the issue was getting their trophies back home to Connecticut.

They drove up to this hunter's camp in Joe's 1965 Pontiac Catalina, not a truck. The challenge was to actually tie them both on top of the Catalina. One solution is tied on the roof and one on top of the trunk of the car. The weight imbalance actually lifted the front tires off the ground [laugh].

At every rest area, they stopped they drew a crowd. Even on the road back to CT, there was a stop and look.

My father also received a certificate from the Governor of the State of Maine, which stated that this was the biggest black bear ever harvested in that state at that time.

When they finally got back to Oakville, they hung both from a huge oak tree in my Aunt's backyard. Word spread quickly, and soon, the backyard and driveway were overflowing with people to see this great event.

The newspaper was called, and they came, took pictures and published a lengthy story about the two great hunters. It was a very proud time for the Perugini family. I still have the bear rug, which was displayed on the floor in my house when we were growing up, and the huge rack from Joe's buck still adorns the wall above the fireplace in his house.

THE SHOOT OUT

When my father was a Carabinieri [A police officer as well as an Arma- a military branch that belongs to the armed forces and, therefore, responds to the Ministry of Defense], he was stationed in San Remo, which was part of the Italian Riviera. He brought my Mom and me to visit on one of the many trips made. It is truly a beautiful place.]

Over the years, we heard many stories about his adventures as a cop in the north of Italy. The biggest story, the one that we still tell people about, was the shootout on the French-Italian border. So the story goes like this:

My father and his partner were made aware of a drug deal that was supposed to take place. They used to work with Interpol, especially when it came to things like drugs. Dad never really gave us all the specifics of the whole ordeal.

Apparently, they were notified of the whereabouts, and Dad and his partner showed up and tried to apprehend them. They were offered hundreds of thousands of dollars to let them go. In the early fifties, that was a huge amount of money. They refused, of course, and tried to put both men into cuffs. That's when all hell broke loose; a fight ensued, which led to a gunfight. My Dad and his partner had taken cover and returned fire. The shooting went on for several minutes. At that point, my Dad looked to his left, and when he did, he saw his partner's hat fly off, and his partner dropped quickly to the ground, thinking he had been shot. In my Dad's haste and adrenaline rush, he jumped up and ran toward the gunman, who was trying to escape over a fence. That is when my father was hit in the side, the bullet going in and out and causing no serious danger at that point. It did not stop him or slow him down. He never lost a step, and he grabbed the runner, placed his gun to his temple and pulled the trigger, not realizing his clip was empty. At that point, he was able to subdue him and turned to see his partner subduing the other gunman. It turned out the bullet only hit my Dad's partner's hat, not his head. All the bad guys were placed under arrest, and my Dad went to the hospital to be treated for his wound. When my kids were young, they used to love to have Grandpa show them his scar from the bullet wound.

NOT ALL THE BAD THINGS COME TO HURT YOU

This might be very short, but I felt it needed to be said because we've heard this phrase so many times over the years. My Dad was always around our family, especially as he got older. He played such a huge role in my kids' lives, and no matter who it was, myself, my wife or any of my three children, any of us was in some kind of emotional distress, feeling down because something happened or didn't go the way we wanted it to go, etc., Dad would sit down next to you, put his hand on your shoulder and say, 'Listen, son, an old man told me one time, he said, Sal, not all the 'Bad things' come to hurt you.' This is another phrase we quote all the time.

NO DEER CARCASS AT THE PARK

It was late November, several years back, at the end of deer season. My father, in his late 80s at the time, was in his garage processing one of the deer we had harvested. My son, Giancarlo, had gone over to see what Grandpa was doing, as they always did, and that is where my son got himself pulled into the following not-so-legal activity [laugh].

As my father got older now and struggled more than before in doing this, my son began helping him. Normally, when we finished processing the deer, what was left of the carcass, we would normally bring it back to the woods. Different animals would feed on it until it was gone.

Since it was a bit of a drive back to the woods and my Dad was more tired than usual, he decided to discard the carcass at the local park in one of the dumpsters. My son tried desperately to stop him and talk him out of it, but Grandpa was very stubborn and was going to have it his way, and now my son was sucked into the whole thing [laugh].

When they got there, there were Moms and kids playing at the nearby swings, and he still insisted. My son kept saying, 'No, Grandpa, we can't throw it in here!' My father's reply, 'Ma, c'mon, nobody's gonna know.'

Well, in some not-so-big enough plastic bags, it went into the dumpster, and my son helped while still trying to talk him out of it. The bags were heavy, and Giancarlo felt obligated to help him, even though he was totally against it [laugh].

Into the dumpster, it went, with certain parts sticking out of the bags, [laugh]. My son was mortified, and when I got home, the first thing he said to me was, 'Dad you are never going to believe what I had to do with Grandpa today!'

SUNDAY DINNER AT VICKY'S

After my Mom passed away in 2014, my father was very lonely and kind of lost, regardless of the fact that we lived one house over and he was always with us.

He used to pay quite frequent visits to his niece, my first cousin Vicky. Vicky's mother and my father were brothers and sisters. She and his other sister had passed away before him. Vicky would call him to come over and have Sunday dinner at her house very often in the beginning. Well, it soon became the norm, and he would go every Sunday. My Dad was also very close to her husband, who always helped my Dad with different projects, and they even made homemade wine together over the years.

Oftentimes, Sunday dinner also included Vicki's daughter and her husband, who had really taken a liking to my Dad, and my Dad had also become quite fond of him. There was also, at many Sunday dinners, an Aunt on Vicki's father's side. She had a very strong personality, as did my father, and this would lead to silly, funny arguments between the two of them.

Following the weekly dinners were the card games and espresso after dinner. My cousin's husband would often send me messages and pictures about the comedy that took place during card games. It became something they all looked forward to.

A & W ROOT BEER MUGS

In 1966, my Dad and his partner opened an A & W Root

Beer Drive-In. It was the first of its kind to open in Connecticut. He spent two weeks in California, training in the management program they wanted you to follow, while his partner stayed in CT and finished up with all of the construction.

They had a grand opening, and the business was a huge success for the two Italian immigrants. They worked long hours, and in a short time, they became very well-known in the area.

If you are not familiar with A & W, they offer a car hop service. You pull your car into one of the bays under a seventy-five-foot canopy, and waitresses, or car hops as they were called back then, come out to your car, take your order and return with a tray that hooked onto your car window. The driver would disperse the food to the people in the car.

The root beer was made in-house daily and served in large, small and baby ice-cold frosted mugs. The mugs became quite popular, and people would very often steal them.

This quickly became a problem, [laugh]. For the most part, the girls or carhops were pretty good at getting them back. The mugs would suddenly appear after allegedly falling behind the seat or magically appearing out of the glove boxes of the cars and then there were the occasions where people would not cooperate and try to drive off with them.

Sometimes, they would drive away with the tray and all the mugs. There were the ones who got away, but if you knew my Dad, however, he wasn't having any of it. The mugs were his property that he worked hard for and you weren't just going to be able to steal them. His partner was more cool-headed about it and didn't go to the extreme my Dad did many times.

I watched him run out the back door and chase after them in his car, and yes, 98% of the time, he returned with the tray and the mugs [laugh]. I also watched him throw a hammer through the back window of a car speeding out of the parking lot with a tray full of mugs. They did not stop, more than likely out of fear.

Dad also kept several big rocks outside the back door for other instances like that [laugh]. One particular night, a van came in with eight guys in it. They ordered eight large root beers. When they finished, they sped over the sidewalk that separated the parking lot area, which was a dangerous move, and proceeded to speed down Route 69. The car hop yelled to my Dad to tell him what happened and my Dad was at the back door like the Flash, weapon in hand. He chased them down about five miles down the road, where he forced them into a parking lot. He ran to the driver's side window, weapon in hand, grabbed the driver through the window of the car and demanded his mugs and tray back. These guys had no idea what they had gotten themselves into [laugh]. He returned a few minutes later with all the mugs and tray, and we all laughed. This story is still being told today.

'OTB' [OFF TRACK BETTING]

I spoke earlier about my Dad's love of gambling, all kinds[as a card player, especially poker, he had a great knack for remembering what cards had already been played], but his absolute favorite was the horses, watching them race and bet on them. Every year, we had pools for the big races: The Kentucky Derby, The Preakness and the Belmont Stakes.

He was a frequent flier at OTB, an amazing handicapper and was treated like a king there. As with him, it was always a fun experience, especially for my boys, who would have to occasionally drive him down to place his bets.

Even after a few surgeries, with his cane in hand, we would have to take him to place his bets. The nice thing about it was if he had a good day, he was always happy to share and hand out twenty dollar bills, [laugh].

When my Mom was sick, he was her main caregiver. He would, almost daily, sneak out in the afternoon for an hour and make his appearance.

Many times, I would walk over to visit my Mom, and when he wasn't there, I would ask her, 'Ma, where's Daddy?' Her response was, 'He had to go to his office for a while,' and she would snicker.

Back in the days of JaiAlai, he even developed a 'system' with charts and graphs telling him which numbers were due to win that day or the next day, [laugh]. I'm not sure it really worked, [laugh]

WILD MUSHROOMS

My father was also a master wild mushroom picker/forger. He had an incredible knack for finding the right spots and would never tell anyone where those spots were. I knew all of them because if he was away and it was the mushroom season, which in the northeast is the fall, I would have to go check all the spots and double-check to make sure no one else would find them.

If, on the rare occasion, someone else happened upon the spots and picked the mushrooms first, it was *not* a good day!

Many times, he would even cover them with branches, shrubs and leaves to hide the mushrooms from other people's snooping eyes [laugh].

My father also taught me how to find and pick wild asparagus, which grew in the spring, usually on the back country roads. I would drive and check certain areas and pick every year until I moved to Florida in 2022.

These were simple and fun traditions, like so many others, that were passed down through the generations. I would even load the car with my wife and kids and teach them how to spot the asparagus. Whoever found them got to go pick it.

[I've made some great frittatas with those!]

EATING HIS WAY THROUGH THE GROCERY STORE

My father had a way of doing and saying things that would just make you shake your head, laugh and then turn and walk away, not believing what he had just done or said.

He and my Mom would go shopping together every morning on their way to our restaurant. It was not unusual for my Dad to eat half a bag of grapes as he walked through the store, or if it was fig season, he would eat half a dozen.

My mother, horrified, would tell him to stop! He never listened-he did what he wanted to do, [laugh]. When they got to the restaurant, my Mom was still flustered by the event that just took place. My Dad would laugh as she told us about the adventure.

TAKING CARE OF HIS WIFE

    With all of the exciting, crazy, funny things that we remember about my father, the part that stands out above anything else is his love for his wife.

    When my Mom's health really started to fail, she required a significant amount of care. My wife and I had full-time jobs and kids in college, which limited our time to help care for Mom. My brother had unfortunately and tragically passed away already. My wife and I did all we could to help my Dad, and he was perfectly fine to be her full-time caregiver.

    As time went on, and she continued to decline, it was very apparent that this was becoming more difficult for Dad to manage. My Mom was no longer able to get up and move around freely on her own.

There were increasing numbers of hospital visits and short-term rehab visits. When Mom was in the rehab facility, Dad was there twice a day, lunch and dinner, to help her eat and then would watch television with her until visiting hours were over.

These were very difficult times and to see his devotion to her was incredible. I would say to him, 'Dad, Mommy is really not going to get better, and it is becoming increasingly hard for you to keep up with the constant care. [Dad even had to have hernia surgery because of all the lifting that was involved from my mother not being mobile.]

My Dad's response was, 'Your mother has been a good wife all these years. I will die if I have to, just to take care of her. How could anyone argue with that statement that came directly from his heart? We just continued on this way until my poor, beautiful mother passed away on January 27, 2014.

.... And then there were two, me and my Dad.

He used to tell my kids, 'Grandma was a bad girl. She left me.' He would always say to us, 'I'm very lonely without my wife. I really miss my wife.' It was heart-wrenching for all of us to see and watch, but he just kept going every day.

My father had a mild stroke right before his 90th birthday. We had a beautiful celebration on his actual birthday, and as we were talking, he turned and said to me, 'I'm not afraid of dying. I don't want to leave you here alone,' [both of us, now in tears]. I replied, 'Dad, I'm sorry, but I'm not going with you', and we both laughed.

As we continued to celebrate my father, we had another surprise for him. Since all the family was gathered under tarps and tents on this rainy CT day, our daughter Isabella's then boyfriend Jeffrey got down on bended knee and asked her to marry him. My Dad was so very happy, and this made the day even more special.

I DON'T HAVE NO PAINS!

My father had dealt with some of his own health issues over the years, like high blood pressure, high cholesterol, etc., as we age.

Kind of early on, in his late 60's, Dad was diagnosed with prostate cancer. In a private conversation with my brother and I, his main concern was not being able to see his grandchildren grow up. Thankfully, he made it through everything that was thrown at him. [Dad had more serious issues later in life- kidney cancer, radiation, several bleeds to the brain from serious falls...]

It was amazing to see the strength and courage he had in handling these issues. The kids thought he was Superman because nothing could stop him.

My father, as he got older, always associated pain with illness [laugh]. In his mind, if he didn't have any pain, there couldn't possibly be anything wrong. We laughed at his reasoning all the time.

If the doctor told him there was something wrong, his immediate reply was, 'But I don't have NO pains anywhere. I feel good, I don't feel sick.' There was no way to make him realize that just because there were 'No Pains' didn't mean there wasn't an issue.

This is another in the long strip of phrases or quotes- Grandpa quotes, that we reference to each other on a regular basis, and we all laugh together.

I CAN'T STAND ON THAT GUY

Another very popular phrase or quote that we all reference all the time is the title of this micro story.

If there was a person that my Dad didn't care for, for whatever reason, he would use this phrase. There weren't many people that he didn't like. My Dad was very social, quite popular and very well respected, but still, there was always that one person where he would just pipe up and say,' I can't STAND on that guy!!' [laugh]

My brother would always turn away from him after he said it and say, 'So don't stand on him then,' [laugh]

When our family is together, and we are talking about my father, this one always seems to come up and always gets a good laugh.

MARC, YOU GOT THE SLUGS?

Shooting a deer or any animal for that fact out of season is generally illegal, and that didn't always stop my father. Back in the 70's, we were all part of a local hunting & fishing club. We used to stock the woods with pheasants, generally on Friday afternoon or sometimes very early Saturday morning. The law stated that no one could start hunting until 8 am. There were several different farms that the club leased, so our members could enjoy Saturday morning hunting with fathers, sons and cousins, and it was always a great time.

My father was the president of the club, and his cousin Joe, the vice president. Being deer hunters we were never without slugs for their shotguns. They were not legal all year, only for a small period of time, maybe two weeks. Nevertheless, we carried them just in case we came upon a deer while hunting for pheasants and rabbits.

One particular morning, after another successful hunt, my father and I were leaving the parking area that we were in. I was driving his pickup truck, which always had a gun rack in the back window. [In those days, it was allowed to have the gun rack, which was quite visible in the back window of the truck.]

We started heading down the road. It was a pretty busy route that connected one town with another. My Dad, in the passenger seat, all of a sudden my Dad says: 'Marc, Marc, stop, stop the truck and turn around! There is a big fucking buck in that field!' 'Dad, I can't just stop here. There are

33

other cars coming!' Dad: 'C'mon, stop the truck, turn the truck around. I can shoot him from the window.'

Me: 'Dad, are you crazy??? You can't shoot out the window here on this road!'

Dad then says: 'Sonamabitch! I don't have any slugs!' [in his thick Italian accent]

I can hear it like it was yesterday. Then he said to me, 'Marc, you got the slugs??' My gun was a different caliber than his and I hesitantly said, 'Yes, I have three.'

He yells,' Gimme your gun.' I reached back for my gun on the rack, then reached in my pocket for my slugs. As I am handing them to him, I'm saying, 'Dad, you can't shoot this deer out of the window right here!!!   What the f***This is crazy. We are going to get arrested!'

Dad: 'C'mon, c'mon, give me the slugs before he runs away.'

So I quickly made the u-turn, stopped as close to the guardrail as I could and kept my eyes open for passersby.

Then I hear, BANG...and my Dad, 'Okay, I got him.'

He jumps out of the truck to go and drag the deer to a spot not visible to anyone driving by. I went down the road, turned the truck around and came back up to the spot where he shot from. Dad jumped into the truck, and we left with some haste.

[laugh]

Later that day, after it had gotten dark, he went back with a couple of friends who also had some experience with this kind of thing, and they were able to get the deer out of the woods and into his garage. Thank goodness, all ended well.

When I get together with some of my cousins, and we talk about the old hunting stories, this one is at the top of the list!

THE DENTIST

Sometime back in the early 1960's, my Dad had a very bad experience with some dental work he had done. He had a toothache for a couple of days, which escalated to the point where he could not stand it anymore and called the dentist.

It was in the middle of winter, early evening, and there was a snowstorm that dropped a foot or more of snow. My Mom and Dad actually had to walk to the dentist's office, which was in the center of Oakville, our small town in CT.

The doctor opened his office for my Dad, and he had to pull the tooth because of an infection of some kind. For some unknown reason, when the doctor finished and stitched my Dad back up to close the hole from the tooth, he left the packing in it! They had no idea that the dentist had made this mistake, and when finished, they trudged back out into the snow and walked back to the house, which was all uphill, I might add.

During the night, whatever pain medication he had given my dad had worn off, the pain returned with a vengeance because the packing was stitched inside. All the aspirin in the world was not going to stop his pain and swelling. As my mother recalls it, he was fit to be tied. Getting through the night was truly a challenge.

They returned to the dentist's office first thing in the morning. My mother said she had all she could do to keep my father from killing this guy, and he assured him if he did not fix the problem, he would return, and there would be hell to pay. My Mom said the dentist literally turned white with fear, and needless to say, the problem had been corrected. My father swore off dentists from that day forward.

It was not an uncommon thing for my father to pull his own teeth as he started to get older, and certain dental issues would arise from time to time.

My wife vividly remembers when he complained about his tooth, and the next day, when he came over, she asked him how his tooth was, and he said, 'I pull em,' proud of his work and that he didn't have to pay for ' a stupid fucking dentist,' [his words, laugh].

There was also a time when one of his teeth had chipped and became jagged and cut the inside of his mouth a couple of times when he would chew. The solution is to go to the hardware store and buy a small metal file [the ones that you would put on the end of a power drill], then proceed to file the chipped tooth until it is nice and smooth [laugh]. Thank God he never had many dental issues over the years!

THE BRIONI SUIT

My father was always a very sharp dresser, as well as my beautiful mother. In their younger years, they looked like movie stars of their era. My Dad always bought expensive

Italian designer clothes and suits that were always tailored to perfection.

I want to say it was around 1973 or 1974 he bought this one particularly beautiful, gray plaid Brioni suit from Italy. The craftsmanship and style were amazing for 'that time period.'

The years went on and my Dad was getting older and was the person that never got rid of anything, including the beautiful clothes from the 70's.

Well into his 80s, my Dad always looked good, dressed nice and was well-kept, but his fashion sense was suffering,

[laugh].

We were now fifteen or twenty years into the 2000s and when we had to attend some kind of gathering like a wedding, banquet, or anniversary, my Dad would pull out the old clothes. While he looked great, he also looked like a walking picture from the mid-70s. It was incredible.

One event, my wife and I picked up my father, and as he was making his way to the car, there it was…the gray Brioni suit, with a bright orange silk shirt from the same time period and a blue tie! [laugh]

Some of my close family members and I would admire his sense of style, even in his eighties, [laugh], in a good and loving way.

NICKNAMES

Dad always had nicknames, especially for my kids and wife. He would walk into our house everyday between 5:00-5:30 [you could set your clock by him!]. He would see my wife, usually with a kiss on the cheek or a rough shake of her shoulders if she was sitting and say, 'Donald Duck' or 'Donatella' [my wife's name is Donna].

When either or both of our sons would come in, it would be something like, 'Hey Luigi, or Scungilli, or Louie, or Hey, Jimmy!'

When he saw our daughter, it was basically, 'Hey beautiful, get over here and give Grandpa a kiss!' He would then always add, 'Look at her, in his Italian accent, she's perfett, she's perfett!'

Isabella's husband used to love to come over to our house. We had a firepit, and he was not one to sit around and do nothing. He would go out back, gather any junk brush or stray branches that had fallen off the trees, throw everything into the firepit and burn, making a pretty nice fire to enjoy. My Dad loved fires, and he would sit and watch Jeff throw everything in and burn it and he would stay there and just stare at the flames.

This earned Jeff the nickname, 'The Fireman'. Every time

Dad would come over and Jeff was there. He'd say, 'Hey, the Fireman is here!' Jeff loved it [laugh].

My son Marco's wife's name is Jesse. My Dad knew Jesse for a couple of years, loved her and wanted to see them get married in the worst way. He used to say all the time, 'She's a really nice ah girl.' The dementia was getting worse, and he started to forget people's names. He used to call her 'Jackie,' then I would quietly correct him, and he would get upset with himself. This earned Jesse the nickname, 'Jackie, the nice girl,' [laugh]. My son, Giancarlo's girlfriend, Rachel, unfortunately only got to meet him once, and he was already in the memory care unit at that point, so sadly, he wasn't able to give Rachel a nickname. [Just a quick mention that both my sons lived in Florida for the past eight years, which also made it a bit difficult to be able to visit as often as they would have liked.]

JARRING TOMATOES

It was a Sunday morning in late September. I get a call from my father at around 8 am. I answer the phone, and he sounds very out of sorts, like he's out of breath almost. Frantically, my Dad says, 'Marc, please, can you come over here?'

Me: 'What's wrong? Why do you sound like that?'

Dad: 'I have been up since three o'clock this morning. I'm trying to make these Goddamn tomatoes!'

I had no idea what he was talking about!

Dad: 'Please, come and help me.'

Me: 'Okay, okay, I'm coming, shaking my head at this point.

What the hell is he doing over there?

I put my shoes on and walk over to my Dad's. I walk in the back door, which is where the kitchen is. All I could see were tomatoes from one end of the kitchen to the other, the counters, in the sink, on the table, on the stove, and he was frantic! It was a total disaster, [laugh]. I put my hands on my head. I didn't know what to say or where to start.

Apparently, unbeknownst to me, one of my cousins was going to Pennsylvania to buy numerous cases of tomatoes to jar for the winter months, as this was a big tradition with the Italians.

Dad: 'Marc, pleas, I got a big fuckin' mess here,' in that accent, sweating and all red in the face.

Me: 'Where the fuck did you get all these tomatoes?' [laugh]

Dad: ' I start at 3 o'clock. I couldn't sleep, so I start to boil these fucking tings.'

For those who don't know how big a job this is when it's time to jar tomatoes. Usually, the whole family is involved in the process. Sometimes, two or more families get together to do this.

Immediately, I jump in to try to get a handle on this disaster. About ten minutes in, I realized just me wasn't going to be enough, so I called my wife and said to her, 'Donna, can you please come over here as soon as you can? You can't imagine what's going on here, [laugh]. My wife comes over, takes one look, is horrified and calls my kids to come to Grandpa's because we need all hands on deck!

Everyone is given a different job to do jarring, one boiling, two cutting the tomatoes, one adding basil and salt. My father was so completely overwhelmed he had to go sit for a bit to regroup [laugh].

It took us at least three or four hours, but we got everything done. I very respectfully said to my Dad, 'Please don't do this again without letting me know!' After that, I also called my cousins and asked them not to bring him any more cases of tomatoes [laugh].

CHRISTMAS EVE E.R. VISIT

In most Italian families, Christmas Eve is a very big tradition of lots of family together, feasting on a variety of different fish. It's an amazing night filled with good food, laughter and love. We spent every Christmas Eve with a house full of cousins and people who had no place to go and sit around the table and enjoy the evening. After dinner had been cleared away, we'd have espresso and all kinds of desserts. My cousins still talk about the fact that my Mom would have us all singing Christmas carols for a good part of the night.

One particular Christmas Eve, my kids were still pretty young, especially my daughter. She was trying to open a present, but the actual doll was secured to the box with those hard, plastic ties. My Dad was trying to cut it loose for her with a knife. Well, the knife slipped and cut my father's hand pretty significantly/ he cut a capillary, I think they later told us. The blood was squirting straight up and out of his hand. He was trying to stop it, but to no avail, and we all tried, but my brother and I made the executive decision to bring him to the emergency room.

Thankfully, when we arrived, there was no one in there! I guess Christmas Eve is a good time for an ER visit [laugh]. We were taken very quickly back to the rooms and the doctor showed up literally within a couple of minutes. We all had some great conversations about this event and shared a few laughs together.

They were able to stop the bleeding, and my Dad received five stitches. One person who helped was a male nurse. He was a really nice guy and enjoyed his time with my Dad. He clearly understood my Dad's personality. Nevertheless, he was cleaned up and stitched up, and we were at the door in an amazing forty-five minutes.

I ran into the same male nurse about two weeks later at the video store. He asked me how my Dad was doing with a laugh. I said, 'He's good. He took the stitches out himself about a week ago.' He laughed and said, 'That doesn't surprise me at all.'

We used to ask each other all the time, does this guy even feel pain??? [laugh]

FATHER'S DAY MARTINIS

It was Father's Day, and I don't remember the exact year, possibly 2015. Our daughter ended up in the emergency room from abdominal pain, and doctors were running tests. It was my Dad, my wife, and my eldest son Marco; our younger son, Giancarlo, was in the army, stationed in Hawaii at the time.

Since we spent many hours of our time there, my wife suggested we stop for a drink to celebrate at a local restaurant/bar in town to try and salvage what was left of Father's Day. My wife stayed with Isabella as they were admitting her.

My Dad, my son and I sat at the bar and ordered martinis. We got into conversation and spent a very nice two hours or so just chatting about life and things that just happened and how to handle them. We hadn't eaten dinner, and after two martinis on an empty stomach, my Dad was feeling no pain [laugh].

As we walked to the car, the now very happy old man kept repeating to us, 'Oh my God, that was the best Father's Day I ever had!'. He was so happy AND tipsy that he must have repeated it four or five times by the time we got him home. I suggested to my son that he walk Grandpa inside to make sure he gets in safely, and of course, he tells Marco that he's a 'good boy' as they make their way in. It was a very happy couple of quality hours at the end of a very long day.

THE DOGS IN ITALY EAT EVERYTHING

Sal and Mia

As my kids were all grown and my Dad was getting older, my son Giancarlo and daughter Isabella decided to come home one day with a dog-a four-month-old, white, full-bred Siberian husky and named her MIA. She is a beautiful dog, but I was not happy about this at all. Along with my very long work hours and my wife's hours, I did not want to get stuck taking care of her. I have to give them credit, though. They were very good at taking responsibility and caring for her.

My Dad was also not a fan of dogs in the house. Growing up, we always had dogs. However, the difference was they were not really pets; they were bred for hunting, and that's pretty much what they did.

Without getting into all the details, Mia was not supposed to be fed table food or scraps. We did give her certain fruits or samples and treats from time to time, but as she was growing, the kids tried to keep her on a pretty strict diet and schedule.

Now, mind you, my father *loved* this dog, and Mia was always so excited she would tinkle on the spot because she loved him too.

It became a constant struggle with Dad sneaking treats under the table to Mia- things like, oh, I don't know, pork chop bones, clams with garlic, bread dipped in whatever kind of sauce was being served that night, [laugh], pieces of meat, baked potatoes, potato chips and the list goes on.

One time before Halloween in October, my oldest son Marco and Jesse were here for a visit and went with Isabella and Jeff to the pumpkin patch. They came home and were outside carving their pumpkins, and of course, my father is always where the action is. He was watching them eating the raw pumpkin seeds and sharing them with Mia!

As it became more difficult to make my Dad understand that the dog would end up with the poops from most of these things, he was sometimes asked respectfully but firmly, 'Grandpa, please don't give her that food. We try to give her a good diet for her coat and skin and she gets diarrhea from it.'

Many times, as he was asked, he would shake his head and snap back and, in his famous way of words, say, 'Ma, you people are crazy. The dogs in Italy, they eat everything!' and wave his hand in dismissal.

The reply: 'Yes, but Grandpa, those dogs were raised on the farm and had totally different diets. Mia is a different kind of dog, Grandpa'.

There was just no winning the argument, so it just went on. It did get a bit better when I tried to explain it to him differently about Mia having accidents in the house.

Now, every time Mia, who is almost nine years old, gets a treat, we laughingly remember and say, 'Ma, the dogs in Italy, they eat everything!'

GRANDPA & SAMBUCA

My oldest son, Marco, worked in our restaurant a little more than my other kids because he was the oldest. He was in high school and if he had a day off on one of the days he was scheduled to work at night, he would go for a bit in the morning to get himself prepped for his shift.

My Mom and Dad were there in the mornings like clockwork. Naturally, they were always excited to see one of their grandchildren, and when Marco would walk in the back door to the kitchen, he was greeted with, 'Hey, here's my big boy!' [he was 17], and Grandma always had a smile followed by a kiss.

Dad: 'C'mon, we have coffee first.'

Marco: 'Okay, Grandpa.'

Grandpa made them espresso, and they sat at the bar. My Dad swallowed his in seconds. As my son started to drink his, he choked and stopped, and my Dad laughed.

Marco: 'Grandpa, I can't drink all this Sambuca at 10 am. Grandpa: 'Ma, I only put a little bit,' with a big smile, knowing what he did.

Marco: 'Grandpa, if I get pulled over by the police, I'm going to get arrested!'

Grandpa: 'Marco, listen to me, [in his broken English] if you get stopped by the police, they say some-a-thing to you, you tell them that you were with Grandpa at the restaurant.'

Imagine, it's okay, with his heavy Italian accent and smiles, because Marco was with him! [laugh]

Marco still talks about those mornings and still laughs about his rationale and antics so many years later, like all the other stories here/unforgettable times.

BURNING LEAVES

Every fall in New England, we face the struggle of raking and bagging the leaves that seem endless. My father had another way of dealing with the leaves.

He would rake or later use the blower to get the leaves into a pile, and despite the law that had been passed years ago prohibiting leaf burning, he would burn them anyway. Now, this didn't just happen once in the fall. He was too impatient for that. It would happen two or three times. Thank God we were blessed with amazing neighbors who loved him and understood his ways [laugh].

A few times, I would get the phone call from my daughter Isabella, 'Dad, Grandpa's burning leaves again and the neighborhood is literally filled with smoke and this time someone called the fire department!'

I would say to her, 'Honey, can you please run over there and make sure everything is okay?' Naturally, Isabella would drop everything she was doing and go check on him.

She would find him with that big shit-eating grin on his face.

Grandpa: 'Hi, sweetheart'.

Isabella: 'Grandpa, Dad said you are not supposed to be burning the leaves.'

Grandpa: 'No worry about it, they were only a few.'
Isabella: 'Did somebody call the fire department? Did they come here?'

Grandpa: 'No, I don't see nobody'.

Isabella: 'Grandpaaaaa..'

On another fall day, I was on my way home, coming down the hill, and all I could see was smoke everywhere. And thought it was a house fire...nope, guess who was burning leaves again?? The smoke was incredible, and the neighborhood sky was fog-covered! I heard later that day from some of the neighbors that they had to close their windows, but thankfully, they all laughed about it.

CHERRY PITS

The following story is something that I never knew about until I was in my thirties. Gardens, fruits and vegetables are pretty important things in old-school Italian families. Most of the yards had fruit trees and most definitely large gardens, all of which I grew up with and still have to this day. In our backyard at my childhood home, we had a huge vegetable garden, several peach trees, a huge cherry tree and, of course, a fig tree.

When my parents found out that there were orchards in upstate New York, which was a two-hour drive from where we lived, we would go there to pick peaches and cherries. They would usually make a day out of it and included a couple of families going together, stopping for breakfast somewhere. There would also be some kind of huge picnic lunch/dinner, and you had to have the homemade biscotti for the ride in the car in case someone got hungry [laugh].

On one of our cherry-picking adventures, we had gotten to the orchard and got our baskets to start. Once picking, I'm standing next to my father, and we are picking and, of course, eating cherries and I notice my Dad is not spitting out the cherry pits.

Me:' Dad, are you swallowing the pits?'

Dad: 'Yeah, as he laughed.'

Me; 'Why are you swallowing the pits?

Dad: 'Aaah, I just chew 'em up and swallow instead to bite around 'em.'

Me: 'What??? If you eat a pound of cherries, you swallowed a pound of pits…that can't be good for you.'

Dad: 'Nah, I been doin' it for years. takes too long to spit 'em out.'

Me: 'WTF,' shaking my head, laughing.

When I told my wife and kids what he was doing, everyone wasn't surprised, and the kids were saying, 'Incredible, Grandpa could eat anything!' We always say he had a cast iron stomach or was sub-human.

We really and truly still talk and laugh about these things…

Thank God he didn't swallow the peach pits! [smile, laugh]

THE ORANGE SILK SHIRT

In my Dad's older years, he was always neat and clean. His style of dress had become more for comfort than his usual stylish/fancy dress [laugh]. He did have a couple of silk shirts and a white sports jacket, though. One shirt was orange silk, which was his favorite, and he paired it with a white jacket and black pants.

On pretty much every occasion we had to attend, that's what he would wear [laugh]. It was great, and I write this with an abundance of love and respect as my wife and daughter would tell me that Grandpa looks so cute in that outfit [laugh]. My sons and I, being guys, would say, 'You look good, Grandpa,' and even made sure he wore some not-so-great cologne, but he wore it. Even in his 80s, he always wanted to present well, and he still felt it was important and that was good.

When my Dad passed away from dementia and heart issues at the age of 91 [and mind you, he was still very active up to that point], I sent him off on his final journey dressed in the orange silk shirt, his white jacket and black pants along with a .30 caliber bullet casing, a $20 dollar bill and a bank pen, which he always carried.

THE FIG TREE

Fig trees are an essential part of immigrant Italian families, as were other fruit trees, but the fig tree is the KING of all fruit trees. They do require quite a bit of work in the fall, however, if they are planted in the ground. Some people have them in huge pots, like myself, here in Florida. The potted ones, obviously, don't get as big, nor does the fruit, but they are easier to care for, as you can wheel them into a garage when it gets cold.

My father had a huge fig tree that was in the ground in the backyard, and it yielded a lot of much bigger, delicious figs. That's why I wanted a replica of my father's tree. There were certain people who would even stop by my Dad's house when they were not home and pick and take all the figs. That's how good they were. It got to the point where I put up a sign in front of the fig tree that said, *'Please, don't Pick the figs'* [laugh].

Finally, one year later, I asked my Dad if he could take a piece of his tree, start it and plant it in my yard, and of course, he was happy to do it. He took a piece of the tree and rooted it, which process takes time to do, but it was spring, flowers were blooming, and the planting and growing season had begun.

My wife had several flower beds in different parts of our backyard that she used to take pride in and take good care of of, [she was very proud of her flower beds and something was always blooming with the change in the seasons.]

My father and I never really discussed the actual location in my yard where the fig tree would be planted. Donna's flower beds, my vegetable garden and an area where we had our fire pit already had their places in our yard.

My Dad had never told me that the fig tree was ready to be planted. On a very nice spring Saturday morning, around 7:30 in the morning, my wife was looking out our kitchen window with a view of our backyard, enjoying her cup of coffee. Suddenly, she calls up to me in a very perplexed voice: 'Mmaaaarrrc...'

Me: 'Yes honey, what is it?'

Donna: 'Can you come down here, please? Your father and Uncle Nunzi are in the flower bed near the garage, and they are pulling out all my flowers!'

Me: 'WTF? It's 7:30 in the morning, what are they doing?' Donna: 'Marc, they're pulling out all my flowers!! Can you please go see what they are doing? OMG!'

I walk out the backdoor into the yard, 'Dad, what the hell are you doing?'

He and my Uncle turn back at me with smiles, 'We plant a da fig tree...'

Me: 'Those are Donna's flowers Dad.' Dad: 'Ma, no worry, they grow back.'

SMH, I walk over to them, and it's already in the ground, and my Dad and Uncle are very proud of their work. After many discussions with my wife, the fig tree stayed there for a couple of years before I transplanted it.

I was so afraid of killing it when I dug it up and was stressing a lot. It was on my mind so much that I had a dream that my grandfather, Orazio, was helping me dig it up. I took that as a sign and finally relocated it close to my vegetable garden.

Years later, we had a similar occurrence. We had an open space in the corner of our yard. Above us was a hill where the road came down, and you could see directly into our yard because it was at the bottom of the hill. My wife and I had talked about putting a tree there that would block out the view from the top of the hill. Donna wanted some kind of weeping willow. We kind of forgot about the conversation for a while, but my Dad must have been there when we discussed it because we came home from work and we had a peach tree planted in that corner!!! [Laugh] Even though it wasn't what my wife had wanted, we had many years of enjoyment in picking tons of peaches.

My wife loves telling this story, as it's just another classic from the life of my Dad.

I LIKE YOU BOB

It was Christmas 2020, right before everything started to turn for the worse. My Dad was now 89. We were invited for Christmas day dinner at my son-in-law's mother and step dad's house, Jo-Anne and Bob.

Our oldest sons, Marco and Jesse, were here for the holiday from Florida, and we were just planning on staying home and having dinner with them and my father, as Isabella would be with Jeff's family. We were delighted to all be together.

It was a beautiful day; we had an amazing dinner, lots of great conversation and some laughs, along with a little wine as well.

They really wanted to have Grandpa there, as that's what we all called him, as they knew what a huge role he played in our lives.

As the food began to settle and the evening started to wind down, it was time for the drive home.

We stood in the kitchen and took a couple of final photos before saying our very long Italian goodbyes and thank yous.

My Dad shakes hands with Bob and grabs him by the arm. Bob gave him a big smile and said, 'Merry Christmas and thank you for coming, Grandpa'. Dad's responds with a big smile, 'I like you, Bob, you're a nice ah guy'. [laugh]

In reading this book, as you have read, hence the idea behind it is the way my Dad used to do things and his delivery of what he wanted to say.[laugh]

To this day, every time I see Bob, I greet him with, 'I like you

Bob, you're a nice guy. [laugh]

SNOW ON THE SATELLITE DISH

At some point, I don't know why. My father was talked into buying a satellite dish and living in New England. Heavy snow can interfere with the signal of the satellite. At the time, my mother was still alive and not mobile at all, so all she had to do was be able to watch her TV.

It was a snowy winter day, and my wife and daughter were coming up the road, and Isabella suddenly yelled out, 'Mommy, Grandpa's on the roof, Grandpa is on the roof!' [laugh]. My wife stops and pulls her car over to see what is going on. She gets up the stairs and along the side of the house and, stands by the ladder and says, 'Dad what are you doing up there?'

My Dad, now in his mid-eighties, turns and smiles down at my wife and says, 'The Goddamn snow was covering the dish, and Gramma can't watch her cowboy shows' [laughs]. My wife: 'Are you done? You can get hurt and fall!' Dad: 'Ah, no worry about it.'

My wife just shook her head as he climbed down the ladder and went inside to check to make sure the television was working again. My wife got back in her car with frustration and she and Isabella could not believe what they saw, but that was Grandpa.

When she got into the house, she called to tell me what had happened. I am sitting here laughing as I am writing, seeing the image of my father in my mind and hearing his voice explaining the situation.

MAKING MEATBALLS IN ASSISTED LIVING

At my Dad's age of 91, I, unfortunately, had to make the hardest decision of my life. I had to admit my Dad into an assisted living facility, specifically in the locked memory care unit. After going through many unsafe and challenging ordeals, Dad was diagnosed with dementia with aggressive behaviors, which I will speak about later in this book.

After about four months of residency at the assisted living facility called The Ivy, my father finally adjusted to this major change. It was an amazing place, and the people there became our family.

They were having some kind of event. I don't recall exactly what, but the woman in charge of the activities came and asked me for the recipe that we used in our restaurant to make meatballs. I was happy to share it with her.

The day of the event came, and they began cooking and brought my Dad into the kitchen to help prepare whatever they were making.

They put Dad in charge of making the meatballs from the recipe I gave her. At this point, he was pretty far into the non-reality of the dementia piece. However, when they put the huge stainless steel bowl of the ground meat mixture in

front of him, they were amazed at how quickly he just jumped into action, mixing and rolling the meatballs like he had done it the day before, not losing a step. The whole staff was mazed at what they called 'muscle memory' when it came to cooking.

They took several pictures of him with a huge smile on his face, proud and skilled as ever. Maybe it was the familiarity that just automatically kicked in, maybe not, but the look on his face said it all that day, and it was one of the happier memories we have of that terrible dark season of his life.

THE UGLY WORLD OF DIMENTIA

Marco and Dad at the Ivy Assisted Living

For those who haven't had a family member or loved one with this incredibly horrific illness, I pray that you may never have to experience this in your lifetime. For those who know the ugliness of this disease, my heart is with you as you navigate and struggle through with the person you love.

As my father extended into his late eighties, he began to get forgetful, which seems normal as you continue to age. It seemed the last three or four years of his life it came on pretty fast.

At that time, my Dad and I had many discussions about his forgetfulness. Things like names, places and even when it came to doing things like writing a check became a challenge for him. He would say to me quite often as time went on that he was starting to forget a lot and still, we just thought it was old age. He started buying and taking vitamins that were supposed to help with memory loss [not sure if they helped].

Dad still lived alone in his own house, one house over from me on the street, still drove, shopped, cooked, played cards every morning and made his garden. I prepped his medications for the week every Sunday morning to ensure that he was not confused about what he was taking and making sure he was actually taking them. We also made sure that he was eating because, at times, he couldn't remember, so we cooked and brought it to him, or he ate a meal with us.

Along came the day that he had a very bad fall down the stairs in his house. I feel that this accident was the beginning of the end for my father. He cracked two vertebrae in his lower back, a pelvic fracture, and a bleed on the brain.

He lost his cell phone in the fall but somehow managed to get himself to the front door of the house on his knees and call out for help. A landscaper, going to cut the lawn across the street from my Dad's house, saw and heard him and ran over there and then came to my house when my Dad told him.

I lived next door.

I had just walked into my house from work when I heard the banging at my door. I ran over to my father's, got him into a chair and immediately called 911.

When he arrived at the hospital, it was not good, and he was in excruciating pain. He could not remember what happened or how it happened and we did not expect him to even make it through this.

But my kids didn't call him *'Superman'* for nothing. Grandpa managed to pull through, but he wouldn't be the same after this. I'm not sure if it was the trauma of the fall or the pretty large, extensive brain bleed that seemed to kick the dementia into full speed. Dad spent weeks in the hospital and three weeks in rehab, all of this as Covid was in full bloom.

I am not going to get into all the details of everything that happened in the last two years. What I will say is that dementia has an incredible way of turning its victims into a person you never knew or recognized.

There has to be incredible amounts of patience, understanding and love, and your loved ones have to be cared for, and safe. These become the major priorities.

What you have to know or come to understand is that the person you once knew, whether it be your mother, father, brother, sister, aunt, uncle, cousin or friend, no longer really lives in that body. Their reality is not the same as yours.

They will do and say things you've never imagined, sometimes very hurtful to the caregivers, but you must have empathy and understand that this is not the same person and they are in a different place mentally.

I never really saw dementia until it happened to my Dad. In the beginning stages, during moments of clarity, you don't recognize it unless you spend a lot of time with the person.

My father knew something was wrong, and he shared that he had trouble remembering things. I had to tape written notes of reminders all around his house so he wouldn't forget to shut the stove off, the dryer off, the lights off, not light any candles, etc.

We found later that he hid a lot. I cannot imagine his fears as he fought hard to beat this beast. We found phone numbers, addresses and names taped to the headboard of his bed, along with books about the mind under his bed.

My father was diagnosed with *Dementia with Behavioral Disturbances*. He always had a strong personality but was never ever angry or violent in any way. He loved his family. That's what made it so hard to understand; how could he say all those things to me, I thought?

One night, while my father was in the hospital, trying to get his medications straightened out, a very compassionate psychiatric doctor called and talked to me and my wife. I will never forget that conversation and how it cleared up so many things for me. [Don't be afraid to reach out.] It didn't necessarily make it easier to hear these things, but it gave me a better understanding.

With that consult and help from my wife, who had the knowledge and worked caring for the elderly as a CNA in her earlier years, and is stronger than me in so many ways and held me up through this incredible nightmare.

There were so many nights I went home, sitting with my head in my hands, saying, 'I can't do this anymore.' She would sit with me and say, 'Yes, you can. You are stronger than you think. God is with you, and you are all he has left.

You *have* to do it. And **WE** did.

The decision to finally have to move him to assisted living was so difficult. No one ever wants to make the decision to take someone out of their home, but it becomes a matter of safety for them and others around them. You never know what can happen, and after a series of mishaps, accidents and very close calls, the choice becomes clear.

We decorated his apartment in the memory care unit with all the things from his home to make him feel familiar and safe: chairs, tables, lamps, pictures, his bed, and bedding, right down to his pictures on the refrigerator, we made a mini version of his house.

Dad spent his last nine months here, and the first few months were not easy and very confusing and unsettling for him. He suffered a heart attack there, a big setback that took weeks to get back on track and then another mini-stroke, another setback. Finally, we seemed to hit a groove, and the doctors were able to get his medications regulated, and he was doing okay.

I left my job during COVID-19 because it had become undoable, and taking care of my Dad became my new job. I visited him every day, usually at lunchtime, as evenings were tricky because of sundowning. For those who are not familiar with sundowning, it is an intensified time of confusion that occurs later in the day through the evening.

It was rare that I wasn't there every day. My wife was there four or five times a week, and our daughter visited frequently, sometimes with her husky, Mia. [He loved that dog]. We would often Facetime our sons in Florida so they could also see and talk to Grandpa.

My Dad contracted Covid sometime in late December 2021. He seemed to handle it okay; he wasn't very ill, and obviously, we could not visit for several days, but he never bounced back 100% like he had done so many other times during his life. He had beaten prostate and kidney cancer, a broken hip, vascular issues, bleeds on the brain, and nothing 6

could take him out. At this point, his heart had weakened even more.

My father passed away at 9:25 am on February 22, 2022, in St. Mary's Hospice Unit. My wife and I were by his side, each holding one of his hands, as he drifted off peacefully right before our eyes. Neither of us had actually been with anyone when they passed. It's a very distinct experience. While extremely sad and heartbreaking, there was also a certain peace that came over us. This horrible dark ride through dementia was over. My Dad was finally at peace with the Lord and my mother and brother.

CONCLUSION

    I sincerely hope that everyone who chose to pick up this book enjoyed reading all of these stories as much as I enjoyed writing them. I felt compelled to share some highlights of an amazing life and an amazing man I had the privilege of calling Dad.

These stories only scratch the surface of his incredible life and journey. A life envied by many, he chose to do things his way, enjoyed as much of his time here as he could, and made it pleasurable for all of us around him.

Dad was very well-liked and highly respected by all who knew him, and he returned respect as well.

I tried to share some of the funny, crazy side, as well as the very human and loving side of my Dad, and it is my hope that it all came through to those reading the way I intended it to.

A TRIBUTE TO MY FATHER/ EVERYTHING IS ITALIAN

(Left to right) Grandpa, Isabella, Donna, Marco, Marco Anthony and Giancarlo

MARCO PERUGINI

74

www.ingramcontent.com/pod-product-compliance
Lightning Source LLC
Chambersburg PA
CBHW070932120626
46546CB00004B/1391

* 9 7 8 1 9 6 5 1 4 6 1 1 8 *